LONDON
Wit & Humour

LONNIE BRIDGE

BRADWELL
BOOKS

Published by Bradwell Books

9 Orgreave Close Sheffield S13 9NP

Email: books@bradwellbooks.co.uk

Compiled by Lonnie Bridge

British Library Cataloguing in Publication Data: a catalogue record for
this book is available from the British Library.

1st Edition

ISBN: 9781909914445

Print: Gomer Press, Llandysul, Ceredigion SA44 4JL
Design by: jenksdesign@yahoo.co.uk/07506 471162
Illustrations: ©Tim O'Brien 2014

An American was taking a taxi tour of London and was in a hurry to see as much as possible. As they went past the Tower of London, the cabbie explained what it was and that construction started in 1346 and it was completed in 1412.

The American replied, "What, a little ol' tower like that? In Houston we'd have that thing up in two weeks!"

House of Parliament next - Started construction in 1544, completed 1618. "Huh! We put up bigger buildings like that in the US all the time – and they take less time to build!"

As they passed Westminster Abbey, the taxi driver was silent. "Whoah! What's that over there?"

"Blowed if I know, wasn't there yesterday..."

8 signs you've lived in London too long

1. You say 'mate' constantly

2. You think it is perfectly O.K to pay over £3 for a pint.

3. You have no idea where the North is.

4. The countryside makes you nervous.

5. Somebody speaks to you on the tube and it makes you feel uncomfortable.

6. You talk in postcodes. "Wow, it was really crowded around SW1 last week"

7. You can't remember the last time you got up to 30 mph in your car in the city.

8. You didn't realise that 'Paddington Green' is real.

A man from Hoxton went into a hardware store and asked to buy a sink.

"Would you like one with a plug?" asked the assistant. "Don't tell me they've gone electric!" said the man.

A labourer shouted up to his roofer mate on top of an old house in Bexley, saying, "Don't start climbing down this ladder, Burt." "Why not?" Burt called back. "Cos I moved it five minutes ago!' replied his mate.

A lion in the London Zoo was lying in the sun licking its paws enthusiastically when a visitor turned to the zoo keeper and said, "He's an easy going old thing, isn't it?"

"Not at all," said the keeper, "He's the fiercest animal in the zoo. Just an hour ago, he dragged a man visiting from up North into the cage and completely devoured him.'

"It seems almost impossible when you look at him now," said the astonished visitor, "but why is he lying there licking his paws?"

"The poor thing is trying to get the taste out of its mouth."

Andy and Martin were delighted that they had finished a jigsaw puzzle in record time and told Louise that the hundred pieces had only taken them six months to fit together. Their friend Louise was unimpressed and said that it sounded like a long time to finish a jigsaw puzzle. "Not at all" replied Andy, "It said on the box three to five years."

What do you do if you're driving your car around central London and you see a space man?

Park in it, man.

One day, a family went into a large department store in a posh part of London. After looking around for a while, they headed for the large counter at the front of the store. This is when they noticed a seal standing in a corner near the counter. He appeared to be dressed in an eighteenth century English gentleman's outfit and nodded frequently as customers' purchases were packaged. The family put their purchases on the counter. Each time the things were bagged up, the seal nodded as if in agreement. After the third purchase was made, the mum asked the counter assistant why the seal nodded each time a purchase was made. "Oh, I'm surprised you have to ask" the counter assistant replied, "He's our seal of approval."

An American tourist hailed a taxi in London and asked the driver to take him around some famous sights.

On the way, a car whizzed past and the tourist reacted, "Look! A Cadillac - made in the USA! Very fast!"

Soon after this, another car zipped past the taxi. "Look! Chevrolet - Made in the US of A! Very fast!"

Yet another car zipped by, and the tourist said, "Buick - Made in the USA! Lightning quick!"

The taxi driver, who was 100% Cockney, was starting to get a little annoyed that the American-made cars were passing him by.

But yet another one did it as they were turning into the tourist's first stop. 'Oh! Lexus - Made in the USA! Very rapid!"

The taxi driver stopped the car outside Buckingham Palace and pointing to the meter, and said, "That'll be £100."
'£100? It was just a short ride! Why so much?"

The taxi driver smiled as he replied, "Meter - Made in England. Very fast."

Man on bus: Are you going to Clapham?
Conductor: It all depends how good they are!

Did you hear about the lorry driver from Ealing who was seen desperately chiselling away at the brickwork after his lorry got stuck while passing through a tunnel?

"Why don't you let some air out of your tyres?" asked a helpful passer-by.

"Nah, man," replied the driver "It's the roof that won't go under, not the wheels."

A Swiss tourist in London was finding it challenging to understand the complexities of the London underground map, so he stopped to ask two Londoners for directions.

"Excuse me!" he said, "I speak no English. Parlez-vous Francais?" The Londoners shrugged their shoulders. "There's no point speaking French to us!" one of them said. "We can't speak a word of it." The Swiss tourist tried again in another language. "Sprechen sie Deutsch?" he asked.

Yet again, he was faced with blank stares from the Londoners. "Sorry, mate. It's a waste of time speaking German to us, as well." The Swiss tourist tried again. "Parlate Italiano?" he asked. Again the Londoners met his questions with incomprehension, so the

Swiss man had to give up trying. There was obviously no point trying any other languages with them.

As he was walking away, one of the Londoners turned to the other and said, "Three languages! That's impressive. Maybe we should learn another language."

"No, there'd be no use learning another language."

"Why not?"

"Well, it didn't do him much good, did it?"

Man on bus: Are you going to Piccadilly?

Conductor: I'm not sure. What else is there to choose from?

My wife saw a brass band playing on the big common in south London.

Clapham?

No, they weren't very good.

My wife went to a dog show in Canary Wharf.

Isle of Dogs...

So does she; that's why she went.

Man on bus: Is this bus going to Kilburn?
Conductor: Only if he steps out in front of it.

Man on bus: Is this bus for Tooting?
Conductor: Well, it certainly isn't against it.

One day, a Londoner parked his brand new Porsche in front of the office to show it off to his colleagues. As he was getting out of the car, a truck came so close to the car it ripped the door of the Porsche off and carried on oblivious to the carnage. In a state, the Londoner found his mobile and called the police. Shortly afterwards, the police arrived, but before they had the time to ask any questions, the man started yelling wildly "My Porsche, my beautiful red Porsche is ruined! It'll never be the same again!"

Once the man had finally stopped rambling and shouting, the policeman shook his head, "I can't believe how materialistic you're being" he said, "If you don't mind me saying, it's no good being so focused on your possessions that you forget the important things in life".

"Why say such a thing to me?" yelled back the Porsche-owner. The policeman replied, "Didn't you realise that your right arm was torn off when the truck hit you?"

'The Londoner looked down in absolute horror. "Oh no!" He shouted! "Where's my Rolex?"

A teacher said, "Do you know *London Bridge Is Falling Down*?"

Her pupil replied, "No, I hope no one gets hurt".

One day a Londoner is taking a walk along the Thames. He sees someone else on the other side. He calls over "Alright mate. How am I meant to get to the other side?" The other one looks back at him, puzzled "What are you talking about? You're on the other side!"

I'd never make jokes about the London Underground - that's beneath me.

Which Lord Mayor of London was always on the Internet?

Click Whittington.

A man walked up to the foreman of a road laying gang in Redbridge and asked for a job. "I haven't got one for you today." said the foreman looking up from his newspaper. "But if you walk half a mile down here, you can see if you like the work and I can put you on the list for tomorrow." "That's great mate," said the bloke as he wandered off down the road to find the gang. At the end of the shift, the man walked past the foreman and shouted, "Thanks mate. See you tomorrow." The foreman looked up from his paper and shouted back, "You've enjoyed yourself then?". "Yes I have!" shouted back the bloke, "But can I have a shovel or a pick to lean on like the rest of the gang?"

Unusual place and street names

Back Passage, City of London

Bellenden Road, Peckham

The Butts, Brentford

Cock Lane, City

Cock Pond, Clapham Common

Copping Close, Croydon

Hooker's Road, Walthamstow

Laycock Street, Islington

The Ring, Hyde Park

Ogle Street, Fitzrovia

Two Londoners were walking around a northern town when they stopped at a shop and looked in the window. One said to the other, "Look! Shirts £1, quilts £1.50, sheets, 50p. It's so cheap here, I'm going to buy loads and sell them when we get back home." So in he walked in and asked to buy 20 shirts, quilts and sheets. The woman at the counter said "You're a Londoner, aren't you?" to which they replied "How did you know?" The woman answered "This is a dry cleaner's."

An Arsenal fan walked into a pub popular with Spurs fans and said "Who wants to hear a joke about Spurs?" A big bloke got up and said: "Listen, man, I'm 6 foot 3, weighing in at 90 kilos." Then he pointed at the man in the Spurs shirt to his left. "And my friend here is 6 foot 6, weighing more than 100 kilos." And, pointing to another tall man in full Tottenham Hotspurs outfit, he adds: "That bloke over there named Rob is a former youth boxing champion. See, you're outnumbered, three against one. So, do you still want to tell you joke?" The Arsenal fan answered: "Well, no. Because I don't like to explain the same joke three times..."

A London man went to sign on at the job centre. The man there said "I've got just the job for you. Can you drive?" "I can", said the Londoner.

"Well", said the job centre assistant "Start tomorrow, driver/conductor on a city centre bus. That means you drive as well as collecting fares."

So the next day, the man got on the road with his double-decker bus. At about three in the afternoon the phone rang in the bus depot. The man was on the phone, "Can you get here quickly? The bus has gone through a shop window, there's broken glass everywhere."

"Oh no!" said the inspector on the other end, "How did it happen?" "I don't know" said the man "I was upstairs taking the fares at the time!"

A man went to the doctor one day and said: "I've just been playing football and when I got back, I found that when I touched my legs, my arms, my head, my tummy and everywhere else, it really hurt."

After a thorough examination the doctor said: "You've broken your finger."

One day a man walked into a bar in Enfield and ordered a beer. He took his first sip and put it down. While he was looking around the bar, a monkey leapt down and stole the pint of beer so swiftly that there was nothing he could do. The man asked who owned the thieving little monkey and the barman pointed to the bloke playing the piano. The man walked over and says "Oi - do you know your monkey just stole my blooming beer?" The pianist replied "No, but if you hum it, I'll play it."

A rather cocky man working on a busy construction site in Hackney was bragging that he could outdo anyone in a feat of strength. He made a special case of making fun of Morris, one of the more senior workmen. After several minutes, Morris had had enough.

"Why don't you put your money where your mouth is?" he said. "I'll bet a week's wages that I can haul something in a wheelbarrow over to that outbuilding that you won't be able to wheel back."

"You're on, mate," the over confident young man replied. "It's a bet! Let's see what you got."

Morris reached out and grabbed the wheelbarrow by the handles. Then, nodding to the young man, he said, "All right. Get in."

Three Chelsea fans and three West Ham fans were going on day trip by train. At the train station, the three West Ham supporters each bought their tickets and watched in confusion as the three Chelsea fans bought just one ticket between them. "How are three people going to travel on only one ticket?" asked one of the West Ham group. "Watch this!" answered one of the Chelsea.

The group got onto the train. But while the West Ham fans sat in their seats, all three of the Chelsea group crowded into the train toilet and closed the door behind them.

Shortly after the train left, the conductor came round to check tickets. He knocked on the toilet door and said, "Ticket, please!" The door opened a fraction and a single arm emerged with a ticket in hand. The conductor took it, checked it and moved on.

The West Ham fans watched all this and agreed it was quite a clever idea. So, on the return trip, they decided to copy the Chelsea fans on the return trip and save some money. When they got to the station, they bought a single ticket for the return trip. To their astonishment, the Chelsea group didn't buy a ticket at all. "How are you going to travel without a ticket?" asks one perplexed West Ham follower. "Watch" said one of them.

When they got onto the train, the three Chelsea fans all crammed together into a toilet and the three West Ham fans squished into another one nearby. The train started up. Shortly afterwards, one of the Chelsea group left the toilet and walked over to the toilet in which the West Ham fans were hiding. He knocked on the door and said, "Ticket, please."

The Seven Dwarves were walking through the forest one day when they suddenly fell into a deep ravine. Snow White, who was following along behind her friends, stared over the edge of the ravine and called out to the dwarfs. From the very depths of the dark hole a voice came back, "Sunderland will top the Premier League this time."

Snow White heaved a sigh of relief, thinking "Well, at least Dopey's survived!"

Why were the Swansea players late for their next big match? They were stuck on a broken escalator!

How many Newcastle fans does it take to change a light bulb?

None, they're all happy living in Chelsea's shadow!

A father and his son, Bobby, arrived at the big match at the Emirates Stadium and Dad suddenly realised that he couldn't find their tickets. He said to his son, "Nip home and see if I left the tickets there." Bobby replied "No probs, Dad." Half an hour later Bobby returned to his dad who was patiently waiting outside the football pitch. He said to his dad, "Yep, they're on the kitchen table where you left them."

Robert proudly drove his new convertible into Bromley with an unwanted gift, a footspa, on the back seat.

He had walked half way around the block from the parked car when he realised that the sunny weather had caused him to leave the hood down... with the footspa on the back seat.

He ran all the way back to his car, but it was too late... Another five footspas had been dumped in the car.

At a pub in the East end of London, a special act was put on to entertain the regulars: a magician. He was a traditional-style magician so he was pulling coins out of ears, matches out of matchboxes and so in. At the end of his act, he said to one elderly regular, "Did you enjoy my act then?" "I certainly did, mate" said the man. The magician replied "Would you be surprised if I put my hand in your jacket pocket and pulled a rabbit out?" "I would and all" said the regular. "I've got a ferret in there!"

A priest was having a well deserved day off by the seaside at Canvey Island beach when he saw two Chelsea supporters out in a boat. Suddenly he noticed that in the water, a Stoke fan was being attacked by a shark. Fortunately, the Chelsea boat arrived and the Chelsea fans pulled the Stoke supporter into the boat to safety, killed the shark and pulled it onto the boat.

The priest beckoned the boat to the shore and said "I've never seen anything so brave. I understood that there was intense rivalry between Stoke and Chelsea fans but this has restored my faith in mankind". He then blessed the men and left. One of the men turned to his friend and asked "What was he on about?"

"Dunno" said his mate "But he knows nothing about shark fishing. Do we need any fresh bait?"

Supporters waiting to watch the latest Leicester City vs. Chelsea match heard that the Leicester players were going to be delayed.

The team had passed a sign on the motorway that said 'Clean Lavatories'...so they did

At a well established manufacturing business in Brent, the young boss had the sad responsibility of telling one of the workers, Joe, that it was time for him to retire after 60 years with the company.

The old man was outraged:

"So, it's come to this, has it? I'm not wanted any longer?" he protested.

"I worked for your father, your grandfather and his dad too.

I tell you what, young man, if I'd known that this job wasn't going to be permanent, I would never have taken it on."

One day a Tottenham fan arrived at White Hart Lane for a big match. He was a little late and the match soon kicked off. The fan was surprised to notice that the seat next to him was still empty. He asked the man on the other side of the empty seat if the person was with him.

"No." answered the man, "It's my wife's seat but she died suddenly."

"Oh I'm so sorry, mate," said the other man "...couldn't you have given it to a friend or relative or something?

"I would have done" said the other man, "But they've all gone to the funeral."

Two blokes from Barnet went into a pub.

The first man said "A pint o' bitter, and a half o' shandy for my mate 'Donkey', please!"

The publican replied "What's with him calling you 'Donkey'?"

The second one said "Oh, 'e aw, 'e aw, 'e always calls me that!"

Have you heard about the latest machine on the pier at Canvey Island?

You put ten pence in and ask it any question and it gives you a true answer.

One holiday maker from up North tried it last week.

He asked the machine "Where is my father?" The machine replied:

"Your father is fishing in Brighton."

Well, he thought, that's daft for a start because my father is dead.

"Where is my mother's husband?"

Back came the reply, "Your mother's husband is buried in Barnet, but your father is still fishing in Brighton."

A man from Twickenham fell out with his in-laws and banned them from entering the house while he was in it. His wife faithfully carried out his wishes until she was on her death bed and then asked sadly, "Haven't I always been a supportive wife to you, John?" "Yes my dear." He replied "The best"." Then I would love it if you could grant my last request and let my sister Sarah ride in the first car with you at my funeral?" "Alright, my dear" he agreed heavily, "But I'm warning you, it'll spoil all my pleasure!"

It was a quiet night in Hounslow and a man and his wife were tucked up in bed fast asleep when there was an unexpected knock on the door. The man looked at his clock and saw that it was half past three in the morning. "I'm not getting out of bed at this time of the night," he thought, and rolled over.

A louder knock followed. "Aren't you going to answer that?" asked his wife sleepily.

So the man dragged himself out of bed and went downstairs. He opened the door and saw that there was a strange man standing at the door. It didn't take the homeowner long to realise that the man was drunk.

"Hi there," slurred the stranger. "Can you give me a push?"

"No, I'm sorry. It's half past three. I was in bed," said the man and slammed the door. He went back up to bed and told his wife what happened.

"That wasn't very nice of you," she said.

"Remember that night we broke down in the pouring rain on the way to pick the kids up from the babysitter, and you had to knock on that man's door to get us started again? What would have happened if he'd told us to get lost?"

"But the man who just knocked on our door was drunk," replied her husband.

"Well we can at least help move his car somewhere safe and sort him out a taxi," said his wife. "He needs our help." So the husband got out of bed again, got dressed, and went downstairs. He opened the door, but couldn't to see the stranger anywhere so he shouted, "Hey, do you still want a push?" In answer, he heard a voice call out, "Yes please!" So, still being unable to see the stranger, he shouted,

"Where are you?"

"I'm over here," the stranger replied, "on your swing."

A man from Wandsworth was staggering home one evening, after a heavy night at the pub with his friends.

He suddenly noticed a man from the water board with a big 'T' handle, in the middle of the road opening a valve at the bottom of a manhole.

He walked up behind him and gave him a shove.

"What was that for?" asked the startled man.

The drunken man replied, "That's for turning all the streets round when I'm trying to find my way home!"

Pete and Larry hadn't seen each other in many years. They were having a long chat, telling each other all about their lives. Finally Pete invited Larry to visit him in his new apartment in Kingston.

"I have a wife and three kids and I'd love to have you visit us."

"Great. Where do you live?"

"Here's the address. There's plenty of parking behind the flat. Park and come around to the front door, kick it open with your foot, go to the lift and press the button with your left elbow, then enter! When you reach the sixth floor, go down the hall until you see my name on the door. Then press the doorbell with your right elbow and I'll let you in."

"Great. But tell me...what is all this business of kicking the front door open, then pressing lift buttons with my right, then my left elbow?"

Pete answered, "Surely you're not coming empty-handed?"

At a London match, a big group of Charlton supporters, unable to get tickets, stood outside the stadium shouting up at Crystal Palace fans for updates on the state of play. Suddenly there was a massive roar from the crowd, so the Charlton fans outside shouted up, "What's happening? What's happening?" The Crystal Palace supporters shouted back, "All the Charlton team have been carried off injured. There's only one player left on the field." Ten minutes passed. Then there was another massive roar from the crowd. The Charlton fans shouted up "What's happening? Our player scored, has he?"

Sam worked in an office in Croydon. One day he walked into his boss's office and said, "I'll be honest with you, I know the economy isn't great, but I have three companies after me, and I would like to respectfully ask for a pay rise."

After a few minutes of haggling, his manager finally agreed to a 5% rise, and Sam happily got up to leave.

"By the way", asked the boss as Sam got up, "Which three companies are after you?"

"The electric company, the water company, and the phone company", Sam replied.

A passenger in a taxi travelling through Sutton tapped the driver on the shoulder to ask him something. The driver screamed, lost control of the cab, nearly hit a bus, drove up over the curb and stopped just inches from a large plate glass window.

For a few moments everything was silent in the cab, then the driver said, "Please, don't ever do that again. You scared the daylights out of me."

The passenger, who was also frightened, apologised and said he didn't realise that a tap on the shoulder could frighten him so much, to which the driver replied, "I'm sorry, it's really not your fault at all. Today is my first day driving a cab. I've been driving a hearse for the last 25 years."

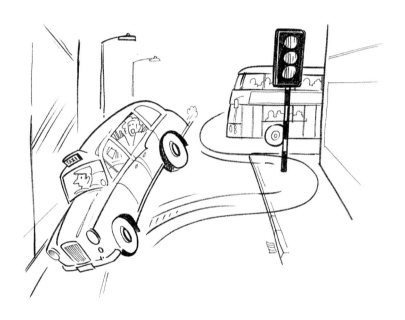

A man from Hillingdon phoned his son in London three days before Christmas and said, "I hate to ruin your day but I have to tell you that your mother and I are divorcing; forty-five years of misery is enough."

"Dad, what are you talking about?" his son shouted.

"We can't stand the sight of each other any longer" his father said, "We're sick of each other and I'm sick of talking about this, so you call your sister in Manchester and tell her."

Frantic, the son called his sister, who yelled "Like heck they're getting divorced!" she shouted, "I'll take care of this!"

She immediately called her father and yelled at him "You are not getting divorced. Don't do a single thing until I get there. I'm calling my brother back, and we'll both be there tomorrow. Until then, don't do a thing, DO YOU HEAR ME?". Then she hung up.

The old man hung up his phone and turned to his wife. "Sorted! They're coming for Christmas - and they're paying their own way."

Jim was having a pint in the Lamb & Flag one night when in walked Simon, a very brash man from Sunderland. Jim couldn't help overhearing Simon trying to encourage some people to bet that they couldn't drink 20 pints in 20 minutes. Despite a great deal of persuasion, Simon was still failing in his attempt to make some money. Then he looked at Jim and said "Well what about you then? Are you interested?" Jim quickly drank the rest of his pint and left the pub.

Half an hour later, Jim walked back into the pub and said to Simon "OK, I'll take that bet."

Simon was delighted at the thought of winning the bet. But his excitement soon faded when Jim drank down the 20 pints in 19 minutes. Handing over the money, Simon said "When you left here earlier, where did you go?" Jim looked at him and replied "I had to go to pub down the road to see if I could do it first."

A man was hitchhiking back to Greenwich at night when he was caught in the middle of a big storm.

It was growing darker and no cars seemed to be coming by. The rain was so heavy that the man could hardly see a few feet ahead of him

Suddenly, he saw a car slowly coming towards him and stopped. Desperate for shelter and without thinking about it, he jumped into the car and closed the door. But then he realised there was nobody behind the wheel and the engine wasn't on.

The car started moving slowly. The man looked out and saw that the car was approaching a bend in the road. Terrified, he started to pray, begging for his life. Suddenly, just before the car hit the verge, a disembodied hand seemed to appear from nowhere through the car window and turn the wheel. The man stared in horror at the hand, though it didn't come near him.

Soon after, the man noticed the lights of a pub appear down the road. He found the strength to leap out of the car and ran towards it. Wet and out of breath, he rushed inside and started telling everybody about the horrible experience he had just had.

A silence fell on the people in the pub when they realised how scared the student was.

Suddenly, the door opened, and two other people walked in. Like the Greenwich man, they were also soaked and out of breath. Looking around, and seeing the man standing shaking at the bar, one said to the other...

"Look mate...there's the idiot that got in the car while we were pushing it!"

A Northerner was walking through the desert when he stumbled across an old lamp. He picked it up and rubbed it and a genie appeared before his eyes.

"You have two wishes." said the genie "Use them wisely."

So the Northerner said "I want an everlasting pie!"

The genie granted him his wish. The Northerner took a great chunk out of it and said "Mmm that's great!"

"I'll have another one of these!"

A teacher at a London School was having a little trouble getting her year 11 pupils to understand grammar, "These are what we call the pronouns", she explained, "And the way we use them with verbs; I am, you are, he/she is" she was added, to blank looks

Trying a different approach, she said, "Susan, give me a sentence with the pronoun, 'I' in it."

Susan began, "I is…"

"No, no, no, no, no NO, NO!", shouted the teacher, "Never, 'I is', always, 'I am'… now try again".

Susan looked puzzled and a little hurt, thought a while then began again more quietly, "I… am…the ninth letter of the alphabet".

A vicar from London was travelling home one evening and was greatly annoyed when a young man, much the worse for drink, came and sat next to him on the bus.

"Young man," the vicar, declared in a rather pompous tone, "Do you not realise you are on the road to perdition?"

"Oh, drat and botheration," replied the drunken man, "I could have sworn this bus went to Chelsea."

A boy from Clapham was getting ready to start his new school term. Because he was getting older and more independent, his father gave him £2 for him to catch the bus home. But instead of getting on the bus, the boy ran behind it all the way home. His father came home and the boy proudly said, "Dad, I saved you £2 today because I ran behind the bus instead of getting on!" The man stormed out of the room, shouting "You should have run behind a taxi and saved me 40 quid you little..."

At an antiques auction in Kingston, a wealthy American announced that he had lost his wallet containing £5,000, and he would give a reward of £50 to the person who found it. From the back of the hall a local man shouted, "I'll give £100!"

A visitor from outside the area was driving around Merton in his fancy new car and found that he was lost. The driver stopped old Tom and said, "You there! Old man, what happens if I turn left here?" "Don't know sir," replied old Tom.

"Well what if I turn right here, where will that take me?" continued the visitor. "Don't know sir." replied old Tom. Becoming exasperated, the driver continued, "Well, what if I go straight on?" A flicker of knowledge flickered over old Tom's face until he replied, "Don't know sir." "I say old man you don't know a lot do you?" retorted the posh bloke. Old Tom looked at him and said, "I may not know a lot but I ain't lost like you are!" With that, old Tom walked off leaving the motorist stranded.

A Northerner was going for a job interview in Westminster and on the way there, he asked a local man for directions:

"Excuse me mate could you possibly tell me the quickest way to Westminster centre?"

The man replied, "You driving or walking, mate?"

The Northerner replied, "Driving."

The Londoner nodded, saying, "Yup, definitely the quickest way"

A man was rushing to a hospital from a business trip because his wife has just gone into labour with twins, and there was a strange family tradition that the first family member to arrive got to name the children. The man was afraid that his wayward brother would show up first and give his kids awful names. When he finally arrived at the hospital in a cold sweat he saw his brother sitting in the waiting room, waving, with a silly grin on his face. He walked unhappily in to see his wife who was scowling and holding two little babies, a boy and a girl. Almost afraid to hear it, the man asked, "What did he name the girl?" "Denise" says the wife. "Hey that's not too bad! What did he name the boy?""De-nephew."

Johnny was down on his luck so he thought he would try getting a few odd jobs by calling at the big houses in Richmond. After a few rejections, a man in one of the big houses thought he would give him a chance so he said "The porch needs painting so I'll give you £50 to paint it for me."

"That's great. You're a life saver. I'll get started straight away!" said the man

His one-off employer handed him a paintbrush and a tin of cream paint.

Time passed and the man came back, knocked on the door and said "There you go. It's all done! Painting completed and finished."

"Great. Here's you £50"

"Thanks very much. Oh by the way, it's a Ferrari, not a Porsche!"

A couple from Lewisham had been courting for nearly twenty years. One day as they sat on a seat in the park, the woman plucked up the courage to ask,

"Don't you think it's time we got married?"

Her sweetheart answered,

"Yes, but who'd have us?"

A man from Kew wanted to become a monk so he went to the monastery and talked to the head monk. The head monk said, "You must take a vow of silence and can only say two words every three years."

The man agreed and after the first three years, the head monk came to him and said, "What are your two words?"

"Food cold!" the man replied.

Three more years went by and the head monk came to him and said "What are your two words?"

"Robe dirty!" the man exclaimed.

Three more years went by and the head monk came to him and said, "What are your two words?"

"I quit!" said the man.

"Well", the head monk replied, "I'm not surprised. You've done nothing but complain ever since you got here!"

A man from Islington was building a garden shed and he ran out of nails so he went to the hardware store to buy some more. "How long do you want them?" asked the assistant. "Oh, I need to keep them," replied the man.

A lawyer from Nottinghill and a cleaner from South London from ended up sitting next to each other on a long flight.

The Lawyer started thinking that he could have some fun at his fellow passengers expense and asked him if he'd like to play a fun game. The cleaner was tired and just wanted to relax. He politely declined the offer and tried to sleep. The lawyer persisted, explaining:

"I ask you a question, and if you don't know the answer, you pay me only £5; you ask me one, and if I don't know the answer, I will pay you £500."

This got the other man a little more interested and he finally agreed to play the game.

The lawyer asked the first question, "What's the distance from the Earth to the moon?"

The cleaner said nothing, but reached into his pocket, pulled out a five-pound note and handed it to the other man.

Now, it was the cleaners turn. He asked the lawyer, "What goes up a hill with three legs, and comes down with four?"

The lawyer used his laptop. He used the air-phone; he searched the web, he sent emails to his most well read friends, but still came up with nothing. After over an hour of searching, he finally gave up.

He woke up the cleaner and handed him £500. The man smugly pocketed the cash and went straight back to sleep. The lawyer went wild with curiosity and wanted to know the answer. He woke the cleaner up and asked, "Well? What goes up a hill with three legs and comes down with four?"

The cleaner reached into his pocket, handed the other man £5 and went back to sleep.

Two boys were arguing when the teacher entered the room.

The teacher asked, "Why are you arguing?"

One boy answered, "We found a ten pound note and decided to give it to whoever tells the biggest lie."

"You should be ashamed of yourselves," said the teacher, "When I was your age I didn't even know what a lie was."

The boys gave the ten pound note to the teacher.

Stan and Alf worked at a sawmill in an industrial estate in Leyton. Alf was known for being very accident prone. One day, he slipped and his arm got caught and severed by the saw. Stan quickly put the arm in a plastic bag and rushed it and Alf to the local hospital. Next day, Stan went to the hospital to ask about Alf. The nurse said, "Oh he's fine, we've reattached his arm." Alf was back and hard at work at the sawmill the very next day.

However, within a couple of days, Alf had another accident and severed his head. Stan put the head in a plastic bag and rushed it and Alf to the hospital. The next day he went in and asked the nurse how Alf was. The nurse broke down and cried and said, "He's dead." Stan was shocked, but not surprised, and said to the nurse: "I suppose the saw finally did him in."

"No," said the nurse, "some idiot put his head in a plastic bag and he suffocated."

A man was sitting in a cafe in Shoreditch, he was fed up and had come out for a bit of company and to try and cheer himself up. He picked up the menu and noticed that it only featured three dishes: meatloaf, shepherd's pie and bangers and mash. The waitress came over to take his order. "I'll have the bangers and mash," said the man glumly, "and if you could throw in a few kind words that would be very welcome." The waitress left and returned a few minutes later with a plate of bangers and mash. She banged the plate on the table in front of the man and started to walk off. "Hey," said the man. "I got my dinner; how about those kind words?" The waitress turned, paused and said, "Don't eat the bangers and mash."